Easter Joke Book For Kids

By: **Mark Alonso**

MW00884319

Easter Joke Book For Kids

By: Mark Alonso

EMAIL US AT:
MARKALONSOBOOKS@GMAIL.COM
TO GET FREE EXTRAS!

PLEASE TITLE THE EMAIL
" Easter Joke Book "
AND WE WILL SEND SOME EXTRA
SURPRISES YOUR WAY!

Why did the Easter egg hide?

Because it was a little chicken!

What do you get when you cross a bunny with an elephant?

An elephant-egg!

How does the Easter bunny travel?

By hare-plane!

What did the Easter bunny say to the carrot?

It's been nice gnawing you!

Why did the Easter egg refuse to be colored?

Because it didn't want to be dyed!

What did the big flower say to the little flower on Easter?

"Hey, bud!"

Why don't eggs tell jokes?

They'd crack each other up!

How does the Easter bunny keep his fur looking good?

With hare spray!

What's the Easter bunny's favorite kind of music?

Hip-hop!

What do you get when you cross a bunny with a spider?

A hare-net!

What kind of jewelry does the Easter bunny wear?

14 carrot gold!

Why did the Easter bunny join a gym?

To get egg-sercise!

What do you call a mischievous Easter egg?

A practical yolker!

What did the Easter bunny say when he met Santa Claus?

Hoppy Christmas!

Why did the Easter bunny hide the eggs?

Because they were a little shellfish!

What do you call a duck that loves Easter?

A quackpot!

How do you know if a bunny is having a bad day?

They have a bad hare day!

What did one Easter egg say to the other?

"Egg-citing, isn't it?"

What do you get when you cross a bunny and a butterfly?

Bugs Bunny!

What do you call a bunny that tells riddles?

A coney-artist!

Why did the Easter bunny hide the chocolate?

He didn't want to share his hare-m!

What do you call an egg from outer space?

An "Egg-stra Terrestrial"!

What do you call a bunny with fleas?

Bugs Bunny!

What's the Easter bunny's favorite sport?

Basket-ball!

How does the Easter bunny paint his eggs?

With hare-brushes!

What did the Easter bunny say to the frog?

"Hoppy Easter!"

Why don't bunnies like math?

Because it involves multiplying!

What do you call a bunny that has hiccups

A hare-larious!

Why did the Easter egg go to school?

To get egg-ucated!

What do you get when you cross a bunny and an onion?

A bunion!

Why did the Easter bunny hide in the flower pot?

He was trying to be "hip"!

What kind of beans do bunnies love?

Jellybeans!

What do you get when you cross a bunny with a magician?

Hare-cules!

Why did the Easter bunny cross the playground?

To get to the other slide!

How does the Easter bunny stay organized?

With a hare-brained scheme!

What do you call a bunny who loves playing the drums?

Thumper!

Why did the Easter bunny paint his ears yellow?

So he could hide in a field of daffodils!

What do you call a bunny that can juggle?

A hare-o of the circus!

Why did the Easter bunny paint his eggs with stripes?

He wanted them to look egg-stravagant

What do you get when you cross a bunny with a dog?

A hare-rier!

What do you call an Easter egg that is always sleeping?

A lazy egg!

What do you get when you cross a bunny with a cow?

An Easter moo-hopper!

What do you call an egg that can fly?

An egg-icopter!

What do you call a bunny with a dictionary?

A word-hopper!

Why did the Easter egg go to the doctor?

Because it had a yolk in its throat!

What do you get when you cross a bunny with a potato?

A hop-tato!

Why did the Easter bunny hide in the mailbox?

He was trying to deliver some eggs!

What do you call a bunny that loves to take pictures?

A snap-hopper!

Why did the Easter bunny go to the doctor?

Because he had a case of the hop flu!

What do you get when you cross a bunny with a snake?

A hop-per viper!

Why did the Easter bunny cross the road twice?

To prove he wasn't a chicken!

What did the Easter bunny say to the carrot?

"Lettuce be friends!"

Why did the Easter bunny paint his eggs in rainbow colors?

He wanted to be egg-stra colorful!

What do you call a bunny with a great singing voice?

A croon-hopper!

What do you call an Easter egg that's been stolen?

An egg-napping!

What do you get when you cross a bunny with a goat?

A hop-py goat!

What do you call a bunny that can't stop sneezing?

A hopper-tissue!

What did the Easter bunny say to the grass?

"Nice lawn!"

Why did the Easter bunny go to the dentist?

To get his bunny teeth checked!

What do you get when you cross a bunny with a frog?

A hopper-toad!

Why didn't the bunny hop?

No bunny knows.

What do you call a rabbit with the sniffles?

A runny bunny.

How do you catch a rabbit?

Make a noise like a carrot.

What did the father easter egg do when the mother easter egg told him a joke?

He cracked up!

Where does a bunny go if you give it a pair of socks?

A sock hop.

How does the easter bunny paint all the easter eggs?

He hires Santa's elves during the off season.

Where does the easter bunny eat breakfast?

Ihop.

How did the rabbit cross the road?

He hopped he could.

What kind of stories do rabbits like the best?

Ones with hoppy endings.

What does a bunny rabbit do in the rain?

Get wet!

What do bunnies do when they get married?

Go on a bunnymoon!

How does a rabbit throw a trantrum?

He gets hopping mad.

How do you know carrots are good for eyes?

Have you ever seen a rabbit wearing glasses?!

Why don't you see dinosaurs at easter?

Because they are eggs-tinct!

How can you tell where the easter bunny has been?

Eggs mark the spot !

How does easter end?

With an R!

What happened to the easter bunny when he was naughty at school?

He was eggs-pelled!

Why is the easter bunnyso smart?

He's an egghead.

How can you make easter preparations go faster?

Use the eggs-press lane!

why was the easter bunny so sad?

He was having a bad hare day.

How does the easter bunny stay fit?

Hare-obics.

How do you write a letter to an easter bunny?

Use hare-mail!

What the easter bunny's favorite dance move?

The bunny hop.

What did the easter egg ask for at the hair salon?

A new dye-job.

Where does the easter bunny get his eggs?

From an eggplant.

What do you get if you cross winnie the pooh and the easter bunny?

A honey bunny.

What did one easter egg say to the other?

Heard any good yolks today?

How many chocolate bunnie can you put into an empty easter basket?

Only one because after that, it's not empty!

What happened when the easter bunny met the rabbit of his dreams?

They lived hoppily ever after!

Why can't a rabbit's nose be twelve inches long?

Because then it would be a foot.

How can you tell which rabbits are the oldest in a group?

Just look for the gray hares.

How does a rabbit make gold soup?

He begins with 24 carrots

Why does the easter bunny have a shiny nose?

His powder puff is on the wrong end.

Why is a bunny the luckiest animal in the world?

It has four rabbits feet.

Why couldn't the rabbit fly home from easter?

He didn't have the hare fare.

when is an elephant like the easter bunny?

When he's wearing his cute little easter bunny suit.

What do you call a trasnformer bunny?

Hop-timus prime.

What do you call a bunny with money?

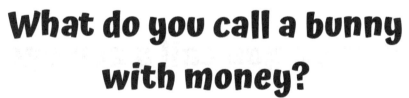

A millionhare.

Why are you so tired in April?

Because you just finished a march.

What do you call a zen egg?

An ommmmmmlet.

Why did humpty dumpty have a great fall?

To make up for his miserable summer.

Why did the jelly bean go to school?

Because he really wanted to be a smartie.

What kind of vegetable is angry?

A steamed carrot.

Would February March?

No, but April May.

How do eggs leave the highway?

They went through the eggs-it.

Why did the egg go to bed?

Because it was fried.

What came first, the chickenor the egg?

Neither the easter bunny.

How do you make a rabbit stew?

Make it wait a few hours.

What did the eggs do on the internet?

They looked for a good egg-site.

Q)
Why are you studying your easter candy?
A)
'm trying to decide which came first the chocolate chicken or the chocolate egg.

Why did the robin save all its money?

It wanted a little nest egg someday.

What did the bunny want to do when he grew up?

Join the hare force.

Where do you find Dinosaur peeps?

Peep-arassic park.

What did the eggs do when the light turned green?

They egg-celerated.

How far can you push a chicken?

Not far, but you can pullet.

What do bambi and easter bunny have in common?

They are both buck-toothed.

Why do farmers bury their money in the ground?

They want to have rich soil.

Why did the robin save all its money?

It wanted a little nest egg someday.

Why don't dinosaurs celebrate easter?

They're eggs-tinct.

Q)
What is the difference between Thanksgiving and April fools day?

A)
One day you are thankful and the other you are prankful.

Why did the easter bunny give eggs to everybody?

He doesn't want to put all his eggs in one basket.

What did the easter bunny say when he was left to color all the eggs by himself?

I'm dyeing over here.

Why don't easter eggs go out at night?

They don't want to get "beat up"

Why did the easter bunny wantto be a comedian?

He was a funny bunny.

What do you get when you cross a bunny with a Kangaroo?

A hooper-roo!

What do you get when you cross a bunny with a squirrel?

A hooper-nut!

What do baby ducks have for lunch?

Soup and quackers.

What do you get if you crossed the easter bunny with a famous french general?

Napoleon Bunnyparte!

Why was the easter egg so strict?

He was hard-boiled.

What do you need if your chocolate eggs mysteriously disappear?

An eggsplanation.

What is the easter bunny's favorite state capital?

Albunny, New York.

Did you hear about the woman who complained about her rabbit stew?

She said there was a hare in her soup.

How does an easter chicken bake a cake?

From scratch.

Where does Dracula keep his easter candy?

In his easter casket.

Why did the easter bunny put a dictionary in his pants?

He wanted to be a smarty pants.

Why was the little girl sad after the easter egg hunt?

Because an egg beater!

What game does the easter bunny like to play at the park?

Hopscoth.

What do easter bunny and Michael Jordan have in common?

They're both famous for stuffing baskets.

Where did the easter bunny learn how to ski?

The bunny hill.

Did you hear about the bunny who sat on a bumblebee?

It's a tender tail.

Knock Knock!
Who's There?
Wendy.
Wendy who?
Wendy easter egg
unt gonna start?

Knock Knock!
Who's There?
Easter
Easter who?
The easter bunny

Knock Knock!
Who's There?
Ana
Ana who?
Ana-other easter bunny!

Knock Knock!
Who's There?
Mora
Mora who?
Mora easter bunnies!

Knock Knock!

Who's There?

Howie

Howie who?

Howie gonna get rid of all these easter bunnies!

Knock Knock!
Who's There?
Even more
Even more who?
Even more easter bunnies.

Knock Knock!
Who's There?
Car
Car who?
Car come and run over the easter bunnies.

Knock Knock!
Who's There?
Some bunny
Some bunny who?
Some bunny has been eating my easter candy!

Knock Knock!
Who's There?
Easter egg
Easter egg who?
You crack me up!

Knock Knock!
Who's There?
Some bunny
Some bunny who?
Some bunny has been eating my carrots!

Knock Knock!
Who's There?
Heidi
Heidi who?
Heidi the eggs around the house.

Knock Knock!
Who's There?
Alma
Alma who?
Alma easter candy is gone!

Knock Knock!
Who's There?
Arthur
Arthur who?
Arthur any more easter eggs to decorate?

Knock Knock!
Who's There?
Police
Police who?
Police hurry up and find all the eggs.

Knock Knock!
Who's There?
Sherwood

Sherwood who?

Sherwood like to ave as much easter candy as you!

Knock Knock!
Who's There?
Boo
Boo who?
Don't cry, easter will be back next year!

Knock Knock!
Who's There?
Butcher
Butcher who?
Butcher eggs in one basket!

More Various

Riddles
&
Jokes

Why did the bee feel cold?

Because it is in the middle of A And C.

What do you do when yourfish signs flat?

Tuna fish!

What did the 0 say to the 8?

Nice Belt.

What is the biggest word in the world?

Smiles. There is a mile between each S.

What letter is a drink?

T.

What letter is an exclamation?

O!

What did the boy volcano say to the girl volcano?

I lava you!

What do you call a door that is cute?

Adoorable!

THE MOON GOES TO THE
HAIR DRESSER.
THE MOON SITS DOWN AND THE SUN
COMES TO DO HIS HAIR.
THE SUN SAYS
TO THE MOON, "BEFORE I START ON
YOUR HAIR,
DO YOU HAVE ANY -CLIPS?

TWO MEN WALKED INTO A BAR.
ONE DUCKED AND THE OTHER SAID,
"OUCH!"

MARY HAD A LITTLE LAMB,
BUT THE LAMB STARTED TO
TEASE HER.
MARY SAID, "STOP!" BUT THE LAMB
REFUSED
SO NOW IT'S IN THE FREEZER.

STUDENT ASKING HIS TEACHER:
DO YOU PUNISH
PEOPLE FOR THINGS THEY DON'T DO
TEACHER: NO.
STUDENT: GOOD, BECAUSE
I HAVENT' DONE MY HOMEWORK
TODAY.

WHEN MY BROTHER TOLD ME TO
STOP IMPERSONATING
A FLAMINGO I HAD TO PUT
MY FOOT DOWN.

PATIENT: DOCTOR, DOCTOR,
I'M GOING TO DIE IN 59 SECONDS!
DOCTOR: HANG ON,
IL' L BE THERE IN A MINUTE.

DENTIST: STOP MAKING A FACE, I HAVEN'T EVEN TOUCHED YOUR TEETH.

TOMMY: I KNOW, BUT YOU'RE STEPPING ON MY FOOT!

KNOCK, KNOCK
WHOS' THERE?
SCOLD
SCOLD WHO?
SCOLD OUTSIDE!

KNOCK, KNOCK
WHO'S THERE?
WATER
WATER WHO?
WATER YOU DOING IN
MY HOUSE!?

KNOCK, KNOCK
WHO'S THERE?
NANA
NANA WHO?
NANA YOUR BUSINESS!

KNOCK, KNOCK
WHO'S THERE?
TENNIS
TENNIS WHO?
TENNIS IS FIVE PLUS
FIVE!

KNOCK, KNOCK
WHO'S THERE?
ZEE
ZEE WHO?
CAN'T YOU ZEE I'M
KNOCKING?!

Made in United States
Troutdale, OR
02/17/2024